THE STORY OF
The First Thanksgiving

This book is gratefully dedicated to Bernette Ford for her vision and guidance.

We would like to acknowledge the wonderful and dedicated performers and staff of the Plimoth Plantation, and give a special thanks to our friend and neighbor, Carol Joder, born and raised in Plymouth, Massachusetts, for her enthusiastic encouragement.

3 3113 01078 8281

Copyright © 1991 by Elaine Raphael and Don Bolognese.

Library of Congress Cataloging-in-Publication Data

Raphael, Elaine.
    Drawing America: the first Thanksgiving/by Elaine Raphael and Don Bolognese.
        p.   cm.
    Summary: Presents the story of the first Thanksgiving as celebrated by the Pilgrims and the Wampanoag Indians. Includes a drawing activity section at the end of the book.
    ISBN 0-590-44373-9
    1. Thanksgiving Day — Juvenile literature. 2 Pilgrims (New Plymouth Colony) — Juvenile literature. 3. Massachusetts — History — New Plymouth. 1620-1691 — Juvenile literature. 4. Wampanoag Indians — Juvenile literature. 5. Drawing—Technique — Juvenile literature. [1. Thanksgiving Day. 2. Pilgrims (New Plymouth Colony). 3. Massachusetts — History — New Plymouth, 1620–1691. 4. Drawing — Technique.] I. Bolognese, Don. II. Title.
F68.R37   1991
394.2′683 — dc20

90-26442
CIP
AC

12 11 10 9 8 7 6 5 4 3 2 1

1 2 3 4 5 6/9

Printed in the U.S.A.
First Scholastic printing, November 1991

44

THE STORY OF
The First Thanksgiving

By Elaine Raphael and Don Bolognese

Scholastic Inc.
New York Toronto London Auckland Sydney

Good-bye to England

On a bright September day in 1620,
the Pilgrims said good-bye to family and friends.
They were leaving England to find a new home,
far across the ocean in America.
There they hoped to be free
to worship God in their own way.

The *Mayflower*'s Voyage

The voyage was long and stormy.
Huge waves washed across the deck of the *Mayflower*.
The Pilgrims were sick and fearful.
But they found hope in the courage and skill
of Master Jones and his crew of sailors.
On a clear November morning a sailor sighted land.
At last the weary Pilgrims had reached America.

Plymouth — The First Homes

Winter had begun, and the Pilgrims needed homes.
They were eager to go ashore to begin building.
On land they found cleared fields

and a deep green forest that grew to the edge of the sea.
They cut down huge trees to make into beams.
They gathered dry reeds to thatch roofs.
Then, on Christmas day, they began to build.

By the Fire

Outside all was white with frost and snow.
But inside each house a fire burned.
The women cooked pottage over the coals.
They patched their worn clothes by the light of the fire.
They kept the little children close to its warmth.
At the end of the day, the fire gave comfort
to the cold and tired men.

A Promise

That winter many of the Pilgrims became very sick.
Some of them died.
Those who could, cared for the others.
They prayed to God for help.
Then, in March, they had a surprise.

Indians came to offer friendship.
The Pilgrim leader and the Native chief met.
They feasted and talked.
Then they made a promise to help each other.
One Indian decided to stay with the Pilgrims.
He spoke English. His name was Squanto.

Squanto

Spring had come. It was time to plant.
The Pilgrims planted peas and barley brought from England.
But they knew nothing of growing Indian corn.

Squanto showed them. He also told them
where to hunt and how to fish in this new land.
The Pilgrims praised God for sending Squanto to them.

The Forest

The forest had many things the Pilgrims needed.
It gave them wood for their homes and fires.
It had deer and nuts and berries.

But the forest was also dark and mysterious.
At night the Pilgrims could hear the howling of wolves.
One summer day, young John Billington went berry picking.
But he strayed too far from the forest path and lost his way.

A Lost Pilgrim — Found

Day after day, John wandered through the forest.
He had only berries and wild greens to eat.
At night he huddled beneath pine boughs to sleep.
Finally some Indians found him and sent word to Plymouth.
Governor Bradford sent a boat to bring John home.
The Indians sang and danced, and everyone exchanged gifts.
The Pilgrims were happy that young John had been found.

The Harvest

The green leaves of summer turned to red and gold.
The corn grew tall. The stalks became dry and yellow.
Plump orange pumpkins covered the fields.

Wild geese filled the blue autumn sky and
brown-feathered turkeys gobbled everywhere.
The Pilgrims began to gather the corn and pumpkins.
It was time to give thanks to God for a good harvest.

The First Thanksgiving

On a sunny October day in 1621, Governor Bradford
declared a time for thanksgiving.
The women and children put pots of pudding
to simmer on the hearth.
Fat geese and wild turkeys roasted slowly over the fire.
Pies and corn bread baked in the outdoor ovens.

Chief Massasoit and his people came with gifts.
Then, with songs and prayers, the joyful feast began.
The Thanksgiving celebration lasted three days.
Everyone ate, sang, and played games.
Together the Pilgrims and Indians lived in peace
and grew in friendship.

Drawing America

You can draw your own first Thanksgiving celebration.
On the next few pages we have drawn pictures of
Indians and Pilgrims for you to copy and color.
You can copy them freehand or use the guide lines
we've drawn.

Here's how:

1. Copy the guide lines — the empty boxes. Ours are blue to make them easier to see. You can use a pencil and a ruler.

2. Draw the main outlines of the figure, copying the lines in one box at a time.

3. Now add the details like those on the pumpkin, the face, and the clothes. Remember to copy one box at a time.

Here's an idea for a puppet.
Cut out and tape your finished figures to pencils or
Popsicle sticks. You and your friends can put on a first
Thanksgiving puppet show!

4. Erase your boxes.

5. Now you are ready to color. We used colored pencils on this picture. But you can use anything you like — pencils, watercolor paints, washable markers, or crayons.

Of the 102 English settlers who sailed on the *Mayflower*, only about 50 were still living at the time of the First Thanksgiving. Some 90 Indians took part in the celebration. Can you imagine how much food they must have eaten during the three-day feast?

The men went hunting to get enough food for everyone. The Pilgrims used long guns called muskets. The Indians hunted with bows and arrows.

The Thanksgiving feast was cooked over wood fires. Here a Pilgrim boy splits a log for firewood by hitting the wedge blade with a wooden mallet.

Watercolors were used to color these pictures.

While the men hunted, the women and young people gathered corn, nuts, and other food.

Pilgrim women wore coifs — tight-fitting white caps —
and sometimes wide-brimmed hats.

Colored pencils were used on these pictures.

The Indian men and women wore *wampum* necklaces made of bear claws, flat stones, and shells. They also carried decorated bags made of deerskin and twine.

Pilgrims dressed in colorful clothes. Red, violet, plum, yellow, green, and blue were as common as dark gray and brown. Their hats often had colorful cloth bands and plumes of feathers.

We used watercolors and colored pencils to color these pictures.

A Note from the Authors

Squanto spoke English well. Where did he learn the language?

In 1605 Squanto was captured by an English sea captain and taken to England. For many years he worked for Englishmen. Once he was even sold as a slave. While Squanto was in England, a terrible sickness struck his people. Squanto knew nothing about the illness.

When Squanto finally escaped England and made his way back to his native land, he found that all of his people had died or gone away. Soon after, new people arrived to settle on the land where Squanto's tribe, the Patuxet, had lived. They were the Pilgrims.

Markers were used to color this picture of a wild turkey.